Plate 1

Plate 2

Your life be bright.
Unto my mem'ry dear
Are friends when far
or near!
Camel.

Plate 3

Plate 4

Plate 5

Plate 6

Plate 7

Plate 8

Affection's offering
Devoted to you.

Plate 10

Plate 11

Plate 12

Plate 14

A token of love.
I think of thee.

Plate 16

Plate 17

Plate 18

Plate 19

Plate 20

Forget me not.

Plate 22

WAR CRY

ECLECTRIC OIL
Dr THOMAS'
WORTH ITS WEIGHT IN GOLD
The Great Internal and External Remedy
FOSTER, MILBURN & CO. Proprietors
DR. THOMAS
ECLECTRIC OIL

Plate 24